Birthing The Vision

Annette Dove

ISBN-10: 0692781714
ISBN-13: 978-0692781715

DEDICATION

I wish to dedicate *Birthing the Vision* to my children: Corey, Raychelle, Kasee, and Michael. I am grateful for my late sister, Patricia Howard Cowan, and my brother, Willie Howard, who poured out their love and support for me as I obeyed the will of God.

BIRTHING THE VISION

CONTENTS

BIRTHING THE VISION

ACKNOWLEDGMENTS

First and foremost, I acknowledge the presence of my God who has chosen me to carry out the task of the TOPPS' vision. It was He who inspired and directed me to write this book. I wish further, to thank many people who played an important role in my success. Some of their narratives will be shared in this book.

FOREWORD

At the age of fifty, I would have never dreamed that my journey in life would travel along so many difficult paths. All I knew was that at this point in my journey, I had chambers–locked with situations that remained untold. *Birthing the Vision* unlocks one of the many paths that came before me. As God takes me to a higher level, the journey seemingly becomes even more trying.

My prayer is that this book will help those who find themselves in a new place of seeking God for their purpose in life. It is important that you understand that God should always be acknowledged, first. No journey will be easy, but if you allow Him to take control, by trusting in Him with your whole heart, and leaning not unto your own understanding; victory will be waiting for you.

Annette H. Dove

Founder/ Executive Director

TOPPS, Inc.

Chapter 1

<u>HISTORY OF MY LIFE</u>

Is serving God difficult? A resounding YES! Service requires obedience and obedience requires sacrifice. However, it is also a rewarding journey if we endure.

Growing up in Pine Bluff, Arkansas, I am the third child born to the late Andrew and Youvarn Howard. I attended St. Peter's Catholic School, but later enrolled into the public school system. My family was well-known in the community. My father and mother were both entrepreneurs. My father was a mechanic and my mother – a beautician. Being young and not knowing the details of private enterprise, I thought we were among the wealthy. Only to find out later, that we were considered the working middle-class. We were taught the value of hard work. We were not allowed much time for playing with other children. Dad and Mom took us on family outings, during the summer, to see and learn the world around us. We hosted family gatherings on my mother's side of the family, and from time-to-time, Dad would invite his side of the family over. At the age of 13, I worked in the beauty shop with my mother after school. My weekends were spent on an Ice Cream truck selling snow cones. Hard work, tithing, and giving were among the values our parents instilled in us. They made it known that regular church attendance and helping others in the community were not options.

My sister Pat, brother Andrew, and I were told that we needed to be saved. Scared to death not to get off the "mourner's bench" as it was called, I would just sit there and try not to look at my Dad's face as he sat across from us. We contemplated making a move off the "mourner's bench" during the entire week of the church revival. On the last night, Pat said, "We better get up and join church. Dad keeps looking at us." They joined while I remained on the "mourner's bench." The choir sang another song. I sat there until my Dad finally got my attention. I could tell from the firm look on his face that if I didn't get up, I was going to "get it" when I got home. So I did it... I got up, and I joined. I accepted Christ into my life at the age of seven. In actuality, I didn't know the *true* meaning of the love of God at this time. We were taught that Jesus loved us—but to have known then the magnitude of His love, I would've done things much different than before.

I grew up in church, but it wasn't until I was an adult before I clearly remember hearing God's voice. It was at the time when I became the Director of the Youth Department at New Town Missionary Baptist Church. I had a friend who always shared with me about her relationship with God. She frequently expressed how God spoke to her. I wanted the same type of relationship, so I prayed. I must confess years had passed before I was able to hear Him speak to me and *know* that it was His voice.

On a Sunday morning as I began to get dressed for church, I kneeled down to pray. I asked God, "What do you want me to do for you." The Spirit of God told me that I would be asked today to become the Youth Director. I remember saying, "God, but I don't know what to do!" My mother had served years before as the Youth Director, but she remarried after the death of my father and left Pine Bluff. Still confused about how it would even take place, I walked across the street to church. At this time, I lived across the street from the church. As I entered the door, Mrs. Lillie V. Hayes, who was the president of the Missionary Society, called me and said, "Net, come here! God told me to ask you to be the Youth Director." Having large eyes, I felt like they had popped out of my head. I was in total shock. All I could think was I had truly heard from God. I replied to Mrs. Hayes, "I know, God told me." I accepted the position that day.

At the age of 16, I was married and starting a family of my own. Keep in mind, I knew of God, but I didn't have a real connection with Him... and I began to take matters into my own hands. At this point, I found myself struggling to maintain my family and care for my infant child. If it had not been for my family's support, I would have probably been dead (a locked chamber). When you are young, you think you know what's best for you— which many times you don't. I decided to go against my parents' wishes because I was in love and wanted to get married. We were both young and inexperienced with life. As a result of my immature choices, I ended up marrying someone who was incapable of loving me the way that I deserved to be loved, and ultimately caused me to become a victim of physical abuse and mental anguish. If nothing else, I learned that it is very important when pursuing a life-long covenant with someone, that you are equally yoked with an individual who has the same morals and values as you do.

After going through a rough first marriage, it was only divine when I met my second husband who is now deceased. William Dove Jr. was a big supporter. We worked as a team to bring the vision to life. In the beginning, it almost seemed as if our labor was in vain as we saw the negative changes going into effect within the community. The neighborhood was taking a turn for the worse. Quite noticeably, drugs and violence began to infiltrate the community. William was a parole officer, and he was able to recognize the transformation. The changed community led us to direct our focus on youth in the streets and troubled youth throughout the community.

When I started working with the youth department, God gave me ideas and people to assist me as we structured the Youth Department. We became acquainted with a young man named Rodney Thomas, who lived in a high crime area. We worked with him and he became known as our son. Rodney had a gift from God that was so amazing. He could encourage young people to come to church that we could not reach. Rodney, William and I became a team. Youth, who had never attended church before were getting involved. In order to play for the church's basketball team, the player had to visit the church and attend the activities. We took trips, developed training activities, and worked in the community helping people. As expected, the devil got busy. People wanted to know why we were helping "those types of children." Negative comments were beginning to surface. The harder we worked; the more objections we received.

After seven years as the Youth Director, I resigned. Some of the young men we helped had gotten into trouble. One was killed. We learned later that two were incarcerated. One day, I received a call from a young man who was sent to a Boot Camp Program. His words were, "You let us down." I had not only let them down, but I walked away from my commitment to God. I noticed there were no programs in the neighborhood for youth in trouble. The area became worse and we moved our family.

The Spirit of God put on my mind the following: "[Annette], what about people who can't move?" I vowed to return one day to my community and implement programs to keep youth out of trouble and off the streets. Through the years, William and I talked of a plan to secure ourselves financially. We decided that I would leave my job and develop a *Family Life Center* for the church.

For a start, I made attempts to share the idea of government grants to the leadership of the church. For such a plan of action, I received greater objections, so I abandoned the effort after five years. God reminded me of the "vow". I talked to William, and we began to prepare financially. In three years, I would quit my job as the HIPPY Director and return to the neighborhood. My salary was $56,000 a year. My part-time job and consulting business were grossing an additional $20,000. We started investing in stock trading and it was great. William was actively coaching after work with *Little League* sports programs, and I was traveling on my job. Life was good. Financially, we were almost there. By the fall, my mother became sick. Her illness took my time and focus. She passed on November 6, 1998. The following year, William and I agreed that we would begin planning towards executing my resignation and starting the community program.

On December 8, 2000, I arrived home from working at the HIPPY office. This particular day had been quite complicated. I could not understand why the goals that I had set seemed to be so difficult to accomplish. I loved my job. I knew it was a gift from God. I began sharing my frustrations with William, so he suggested we get out of the house. He needed a present for his office Christmas party. We drove to the Pines Mall and later shared dinner at Red Lobster. As we enjoyed our meal, we began making plans for our future. William asked me what would make me happy. I remembered answering, "The safety of our grandchild and to do God's will." He just smiled.

When we returned home, I had a telephone message from a friend who had lost her husband weeks earlier. I told her to call whenever she needed to talk. I returned her call and spent about thirty minutes encouraging her. I prepared for bed and walked downstairs to tell William I was going to bed. He answered by saying, "I'll be up soon." I woke in the middle of the night to find he had not made it to bed—which was not unusual. William enjoyed staying up late watching television. As I proceeded to go back to sleep, I could hear him calling my name. "Net, I need you." He was lying on our bathroom floor. I struggled to get him up, so I called my oldest son to help. I awoke my oldest daughter, and she called the ambulance. We were informed that my husband had passed. Losing Mother was very difficult, but losing my husband, William, made me undergo a pain as if my heart had been ripped to pieces.

During this time, an ice storm hit our city, and the entire town was closed down—even the funeral homes. There was no electricity and no gas. Because of the ice storm, we had to postpone my husband's funeral. Everything was at a stand-still—including me. This was when God reminded me of my vow, which was to return to the neighborhood. I remembered thinking, "I can't do this now." I have four children to rear and bills to pay. The entire responsibility was on my shoulders. I needed to work even more now than ever. In the middle of the night, God spoke to my heart and said, "You made a vow." I remembered saying to Him,

"Let me work one more year."

I worked one more year, and it was the most horrible year of all. The program that I had worked so hard to build appeared to begin weakening. Problems were surfacing, and the love I once had was diminishing. I decided to resign in April as a trainer for the National HIPPY Office. I cried because I felt I was losing a part of my life that I truly loved. As I later prepared my letter of resignation from my regular job, I thought I would ask for a sabbatical leave—that way if things didn't work out I could return. The superintendent said he was unsure if he could grant the leave, but we would talk. At 10:00 a.m. on the morning in which I was to submit my letter of resignation to the superintendent, something strange happened. I entered my office and prayed as always, "God, if you don't want me to give up my job, stop me!" The Spirit said, "Read the book, *Who Moved My Cheese*." Someone gave me a copy of the book, but I had not read it. "Lord," I said, "I don't have time." A persistent voice said, "READ THE BOOK!" The time was 8:35 a.m., and I began reading *Who Moved My Cheese*. At 9:45 a.m., I had my answer. I would resign without requesting a sabbatical.

During the meeting the superintendent said, "Mrs. Dove, may I ask a personal question." I responded, "Yes, sir." He asked, "Can you afford to leave?" I said very confidently, "Sir, I cannot afford *not* to leave." And this was when my journey began.

CHAPTER 2

THE MISCONCEPTIONS

In June of 2001, I cried as I cleared my desk. Another part of me felt as if something had been taken from me. I assured myself that I was doing the work of the Lord, so surely things will work out fine. "Lord, I'm willing to do this, but I don't want my status of living to change. I want to have abundance." I prayed. Now that I think about it, <u>God never responded</u>.

The Misconception

The journey will be easy and everyone wants you to succeed. Everyone will be excited about what God wanted me to do. I would get much help and the church would get involved.

A Board of Directors, with fifteen leaders in the community was formed. They were people of influence who could understand the vision which I had perceived. The problem was, I never consulted <u>God</u>. The first three meetings were so well-attended we did not have sitting room. Oh, how excited I was. This is going great. I began seeking <u>God</u> for a building. He showed me a vision about an old house in the neighborhood. I shared it with Michael, my son, and we went looking for the house. As we were driving, I saw this abandoned house with a huge yard down the street where I used to live and across from the church. We stopped, and as we walked on the porch of the house, my son said, "Mom, this is it!

Yes, just like the vision." I called a friend who was a carpenter to meet me the next day. He told me the house was not worth investing in and that it needed to be torn down. He had tried to purchase it and the cost was $15,000-$20,000.

I knew the owner, so I telephoned her. She had been one of my mother's clients at the beauty salon. I told her of my plans for the house. We agreed that she would sell it for $5,000. I paid her the $5,000 without considering the repairs. During a graduation party for my older son I was asked, "You have left your job, what are you going to do, now?" Opening my big mouth, I shared my vision, and that was when I discovered that your vision isn't for everyone to know prematurely. If you are not careful, sharing your vision with the wrong people can cause them to interrupt it.

I was approached the next day by a person from my past wanting to see the house so that he could assist me. Not only did this individual come to convince me, but he also wanted to get involved. He introduced me to a minister who promised if I would help people, he would do the work "for free." All I was required to do was purchase the materials.

Know that nothing is free, and titles don't make you honest.

I was excited, but never asked <u>GOD</u> for His directions. He told me that it would cost me about $60,000 to renovate the house. All I had was $25,000, and if the labor was free, I figured I didn't need the whole $60,000. I was instructed to give money to the contractor each week. After spending $5,000, the cost of cleaning out the house still hadn't been covered. The more we tore down rotten walls, the more walls needed to be removed. Before long, I was out of money. So I cashed in my stock accounts. It was never enough, and the work was not being completed. Credit cards started coming in the mail that I never requested. I considered one to purchase the lumber that was needed. I could easily repay it when the grant money came. Ultimately, I used three credit cards to purchase supplies.

The building never changed. I was completely out of money. The credit card bills were coming in — and to add to the troubles — I went to the bank on October 2, to withdraw some funds. I had a two cents balance. My Social Security check stopped coming because my son, Mike, was sixteen years old. I had not paid any bills for the month, and only one stock account left, that I had set-up. After making a $30,000 deposit in the account, the computer selected the stock. We had just gone through the *9-1-1* incident, and I had not checked on the account. I had planned to use the account for the college education of Kasee and Mike. The last statement I remembered looking at had six figures. When I asked about having some funds sent, I was informed that the account had a zero balance. I felt like jumping out of a window; instead, I took a walk and talked to God. What was I to do? All I could hear was, "Whom do you trust now?" You said you trusted me when you had money. Now that everything is gone, "Will you trust me?" Through my tears and fears, the walk back to the house was long. I remembered saying, "Lord, I'll trust you."

All the workers were gone, the money had been spent, the credit cards were maxed out, and it seemed as if I was all alone. I would drop Mike off at school and go to the building that had no walls and floors. By the way, the work done by the contractor would not even pass city code.

My office and prayer room was the second room which was the only one with part of a floor. When I worked on the room, I prayed, cried, and nailed. Some of the boards ended up crooked, but I did whatever I could do. One day I called my cousin, who I considered as a second mom, to see if I could stop by for a visit. I had not shared with anyone at this point what I was going through. I don't even think my children knew the full picture. When I walked in her home, I broke down crying and told her I didn't know what to do. All I knew was that God had told me to move forward with the plan. I told her about my finances and the series of unfortunate events. Mom, who was Nina Clardy, just sat there. I knew she was praying. Then, she picked up the telephone, talked to someone, and asked the person to meet us at their church. Dad — who was Elder Clardy, Mom, and I sat in the church. Elder David Jones joined us later. I knew Elder Jones because he had worked with my birth mother in organizing community gardens. Mom told him of my situation and asked if he could help. He agreed.

We visited my office. The first thing Elder Jones said was, "We need to bless the building and grounds." Upon entering the property, Elder Jones, Elder Clardy, Mom and I blessed the building with oil and prayed. Then, we walked over the grounds and through every area. Elder Jones turned and asked me, "Do you have a truck?" I answered, "Yes sir." He said get some help and meet me at my house. In the back of his house was a storage building. Not only did he fill my truck to the top, but he filled his work truck, which was about three tons, to the top with lumber, doors, windows, and nails.

We had to tear down the fence to unload. When the City Inspector came the first time to inspect the framing of the walls, he looked and said, "This won't pass." I stood there with tears in my eyes; I had no money to pay someone else to do it right. While he was there, Elder Jones stopped by, and the City Inspector explained the problem to him. The inspector asked me, "What's your name?" I was so upset I didn't want to talk. He said, "I think I went to school with you. Are you Annette Howard?" I answered, "Yes." "What are you going to do with this house?" he asked. After I told him, showed Elder Jones what I needed to do. He left but returned later the same day to approve the work.

Elder Jones explained that he was already employed, but he would help in anyway that he could. He brought his workers between his jobs to work on the building. Different people came and volunteered to do whatever they could. Some I didn't know, but we were still quite a long way from getting into the building. Then, I had those who pulled up outside the property to say things such as, "When are you going to finish that thing? You should have torn it down." They didn't know it, but I thought about tearing it down too… at least until God said, "No."

Dad came every day, keeping the work site clean. Then, it was time for electrical work, and I had no money. Mom said she knew someone, so she called a man to meet with us named Michael Robinson. Mr. Robinson was working and living in Little Rock, Arkansas. When Mom told him I had no money, but explained the purpose of the building, he agreed to help if I bought the supplies. The agreement was that he was to drive to Pine Bluff daily and return to Little Rock around midnight to be on time for work the next day.

I still didn't have money for the project. My first donation came from Dad and Mom's church—Unity Temple. Mr. Robinson was told by the city inspectors that since the building would be a business, we had to use conducts, which meant more money. I used my bill money, car note money, and all that I had to buy supplies. Mr. Robinson drove from Little Rock, arrived around 8:00 p.m., came to the building, and worked until about 12:00 p.m. I felt bad that I didn't have money to give him—even for his gas. He began showing me how to run electrical wires and set up outlets. It was my job to complete certain tasks during the day. He would train me to do specific tasks, and I was to have the jobs finished by the time he arrived in Pine Bluff. He always inspected my work when he came. As the work moved forward, it was time to have the city inspect the building. With remorse, Mr. Robinson informed me that his license was not up-to-date.

The plan was to help Mr. Robinson get his license updated to complete the inspection of TOPPS. He gave me the name of the insurance agent who wrote his last bond. I had a problem getting the agent to give me information on Mr. Robinson. Afterwards, the agent told me he no longer wrote bonds and gave me another company which would. This latter company informed me that it did not write bonds and referred me to a second company. This last-named company wrote bonds for $100. I then asked if I could fill out the papers for Mr. Robinson since he would not arrive in Pine Bluff until later. Upon his arrival, he could sign them. The agent stated that Mr. Robinson had to be present and that the company closed at 5:00 p.m. The agent said that she would call me at 2:00 p.m. to complete the papers. I didn't hear from her, and I needed to run errands. So I went by the insurance office while I was out. On my way there, I came upon an insurance company in a shop walk. The Spirit of God instructed me to stop, but I didn't. I went to the bank and to the Electric Supply Company. The items that I needed, I received *free*! The Spirit instructed me to telephone the insurance company I had passed. I called and asked if the company wrote bonds. The reply was "Yes." Having been told that the fee was $50, I decided I would go back. A young lady greeted me; then, she asked me to wait a few minutes. I was shown into an office. A lady sat behind a desk. Her face was flushed, and she looked pale. I told her what I needed, and she asked if Mr. Robinson and I were related. "No," I told her. She then wanted to know how he was assisting me.

As she filled out the papers, and I was giving the information about how he was helping me to get into this non-profit office, she asked me, "What kind of non-profit"? I told her about an old house I had purchased; afterwards, I shared my plans for the house. In awe, she stopped me from talking, moved back into her chair, and looked as if she had seen a ghost. She called her son into the room and said "You are not going to believe this." She asked me to tell her son about the non-profit status of the house. After I explained the vision for the house to her son, she shared that she had two dreams about me. In the first dream God told her she was supposed to help a lady who was renovating an old building. Her son sat there with his mouth open in awe. Next, she told me about her son and how God had healed him. After she had asked God what He wanted her to do, she opened a home for children—and more related ventures. Tears were coming down my face as she shared her story. God put our paths together. Because the boss' wife insisted that she choose, she gave up her job to be there for her ill son. Her son was a seventeen-year-old minister.

I obtained the bond in enough time to have it ready when Mr. Robinson came to work on the building. When one-third of the work was completed, Mr. Robinson moved to Oklahoma. For two weekends, he traveled back to Pine Bluff. Then, the weather turned bad, and we were at a stand-still. Days went by with no work being done. I continued to go to the building, daily. Through my frustration, I would pray, cry, and seek God for the next step.

I started writing and believing that I could get grants to help fund the completion of the building. I met people who promised to help with the project, but they never showed up. Before I left HIPPY, I met a young man from the University of Arkansas at Pine Bluff named Jeff, whom I shared the vision with. He bought into the vision. We wrote grants together. The first grant was offering $200,000. It required that we work with the local school systems. I met with the superintendent of one of the local school districts. He agreed to partner with us, and we were assigned a liaison to link with us.

Unfortunately, the liaison would not return calls nor convey information needed for the collaboration. Two days before the grant was due, the individual appeared with excuses. Jeff and I completed the grant without the input from this person. On the day the proposal was due, Jeff had an important job-related site visit. I was to finish typing the proposal, make corrections, and make the necessary copies for submission. I met Jeff at his office at 2:00 p.m. The deadline for submission was 4:30 p.m. The document had to be delivered to Little Rock which was approximately a 40-minute drive from Pine Bluff. We finished the final few portions of the document and prepared it for copying. To our dismay, the copier's automatic feeder jammed the original copy. Jeff worked hard to get it un-jammed. The time was almost 4:00 p.m., so we called Little Rock to explain what was happening. We were told, "If it is not here at 4:30 p.m., the proposal will not be accepted." Jeff finally un-jammed the original copy and started making additional copies. To our consternation, some copies were blank, and other copies printed only half the information. Frustrated, we decided to take what we had. Jeff drove my car. We had only twenty minutes to get the proposal to Little Rock.

Jeff was driving 100 miles per hour and I was praying, "Dear God, keep us alive." We made it there at 4:35 p.m. The office was closed. As Jeff drove back to Pine Bluff trying to encourage me, I cried. He said, "We'll start on another grant". I didn't want to hear it. I began to think how I had never asked God about His will. That night, I prayed, "Lord, how do you expect me to do this work with no money—and no program?"

The next day, Jeff called to find out what our next project would be. He had heard about a Robert Wood Johnson Foundation program called *Faith in Action.* He located the telephone number of the contact office in Arkansas. When I telephoned and explained why I was calling, the man who answered said, "My God, we were coming to Pine Bluff today to find someone to run this program." The grant was funded for $35,000, for eighteen months—salary only. This grant opportunity was *great*. The funding would give me income and a program.

The grant was written, but it would be six months before we would know if it was accepted. This latter concern meant another delay. In the meantime, I contacted *Reading Is Fundamental* (RIF) to share our vision for "Reading in the Neighborhood." I wrote the grant, it was accepted. There was no money given to us, but we could now purchase books and RIF would cover 75% of the cost, and we would be responsible for 25%.

Our adopted son, Rodney, helped me to promote my first fundraiser. We raised $325 which was enough to purchase books for 300 children. It was very successful, and my spirit was lifted. But the building was still incomplete.

Rodney assisted me with nailing boards and cleaning up lumber. Through his resourcefulness, we even received donated items. One evening, I received a call from a lady representing a government agency. She needed someone to put a Pine Bluff program in place. She had heard about me. I agreed to meet with her and her supervisors—it meant money. The program seemed to fall in line with our mission, so I agreed to take on the task with one condition—the money would be made out in the name of *TOPPS*. Rodney and I developed a support group for grandparents who cared for their grandchildren while the children's parents were incarcerated.

Our first meeting to organize this support group was held at Unity Temple. It did not take long for us to get started. We were excited, and soon money was coming in to help finish the building. Rodney was paid a small salary, and other finances were used to purchase materials and pay laborers.

One of the Board members would stop by from time to time, to encourage me. One day, he suggested a friend who could help finish the building. The contact was made with his friend, Mr. Davis, who agreed to help with the project. He and his employees would come between jobs to help. When we had money, we would pay. Sometimes the work was done for free. Then one day, Mr. Davis had to leave and finish his work with another contractor. We were left without help. I understood that this project took a lot of time, and the building made our efforts even more difficult because of the condition.

By now, Elder Jones had returned from his other work site to assist with the project. We were down to needing sheet rock. I would seek out lumber companies for donations. I was told at every place that they were unable to help. One large company directed me to return four times to receive a $50 gift card. Elder Jones remembered there was some sheet rock he had in a house which had burned. He felt we could cut around it and salvage some of it. It was 12 feet long. Some pieces had burns spots on it, but it was all we had. He showed me how to cut the sheet rock and nail it.

The Board member who encouraged me about the project sent another man named Paul to assist me. Paul did carpentry work. Appearing on the job site, Paul said, "Yes, I do this type of work." But the first question Paul asked me was "Which was the right side of the sheet rock!" I thought, "O Lord, Why me?" I had to go outside and talk to GOD. Paul was faithful; he came every day. The first room we *mudded* looked very rough. It was the room I called my prayer room at that time. We took two weeks to hang sheet rock and mud a 10x10 space. For someone with experience, it would have taken a half day.

I received enough money to pay a professional sheet rocker. The building was finally coming together. I remembered when the building was ready for painting. Elder Jones told me that I needed about ten gallons of paint. He referred me to a painter who had purchased paint from a paint store that had gone out-of-business. I called the painter and asked to meet with him. He told me to meet him early. For three days, I had arrived at his home by 7:00 a.m., but I was unable to catch him. One morning, I arrived at 6:00 a.m. I was parked outside when I explained what I needed which was ten gallons of white paint. He told me he didn't have any. I stood there looking at white paint in his yard stacked high.

Seeing the disappointment on my face, he promptly said he had five gallons that I could have. I took the paint.

Lord, what do you want me to do! Calling a couple of

people I knew, I asked if they had any paint that I might be able to get. When I received the paint, I had four different shades of white. And still, we did not have enough. *How about that!* When I returned to the building, Elder Jones had four, ten gallon buckets. He had a plastic barrel. He poured all of the paint together. We had more than enough and a new off-white color was created. He taught me how to use the *texture* machine to blow the ceilings. I blew everything: the doors, the sockets, and the windows. Oh well - at least everything was painted. We were down to the floors. A carpet company gave me an estimate of $3,000 to lay the carpeting. This price included the hallways and the computer lab. That is when another *stand-still* took place.

Dedril, a friend, who had worked for me on my last job came by the building. She saw how disgusted I was due to the lack of production. She made some phone calls. The next day, Monica, Cathy, and Dedril asked me to meet them at a salvage yard. They had collected $40 to buy carpet. The color was a pretty green plush, just the right size to cover the floor in what would be my office. They talked the seller's original price down; afterwards, they purchased the carpet and two doors as well.

As I continued to ask God for guidance, He directed me to look up a warehouse in Monticello, Arkansas. Someone had mentioned the warehouse, years earlier. God told me to ask for the carpet to be donated. After finding the telephone number and dialing it, the manager answered the call. He responded that the company could not donate carpet because of an increase in the price of carpet. Furthermore, he shared that his father would have to approve any discount. I was told to call back. I called for four days, and I would always leave messages. No one returned my calls. The Lord instructed me to travel to Monticello. When I walked in, I introduced myself and asked to talk to the owner. I was told that he was with a customer at the time. I started to leave, but God said, "Stay and wait." I waited about thirty minutes, when an older gentleman came out. I introduced myself and told him what I needed. I was able to order what I wanted and needed for 10% of the cost I had been quoted. But I didn't have the 10%. I was told I could pay for the order when it came in.

Lord, where am I going to get the 10%. Two weeks later, I received a call from Monticello affirming that my carpet was in. I was excited, but still had no money. I told the owner I would be there Friday. On Thursday night as I was preparing to leave the office, I received a call to come to a local lumber company. A man had a package for me but could not get to my office to give it to me. When I arrived, he said, "God told me to give you a check." It was for the amount I needed for the carpet. *God is awesome!*

BIRTHING THE VISION

Chapter 3

<u>BE CAREFUL WHO YOU TURN AWAY</u>

I now had enough carpet for the entire building. I was excited, even though I had no one who could lay the carpet. Again, I called a few people who laid carpet. Each one came by the building to do the job, but when I told them I had no money, they never came back. Elder Jones informed me of a young man he knew who was a carpet layer, and stated he would ask him to call me. The young man called and told me he would come by to see what I needed. After showing up, the first thing he asked was, "Do you remember me?" "No," I replied. He said that he had come around here [the building] looking for work when he first got out of prison, and I looked at him as if he were nothing and told him that I had no work. I felt bad, but I sincerely didn't remember him. I told him I had probably responded that way because of what I was going through. After I shared the vision with him, he agreed to lay the carpet for $50 a room. He agreed to allow me to pay him when I received the money. This conversation taught me a valuable lesson… **Don't be so discouraged when things aren't going your way that you are not compassionate with others. Be careful who you turn away!**

But the Great Creator, in His compassion, gave me another chance, and I was able to witness to the young man about God. He shared a lot about the pain of his life. He was stabbed by his wife and almost died. He went to prison but desired to be back with his family. I encouraged him to go back to church. After the job was finished, he came by to visit. He returned to church, but his relationship with his wife had not changed. The last time he visited me he shared that his family situation had become worse and that he had returned to drugs. I prayed with him. Oh, by the way, when he unrolled the carpet for my office, he informed me that particular piece was enough for three rooms. *What an unexpected blessing!*

The interior of the building was taking shape. I needed a heating and air conditioning unit which I knew would cost in the range of $6,000 to $8,000. I asked a friend whom I had worked with in the school district to visit me at the building. He wanted to know why I had selected this building. He said, "You probably need to tear it down." I asked if he could assist me with getting a heating and air conditioning unit. He said, "I only work on them." So back to God I went in prayer. I had purchased two units from a local company and knew the owner by name. God urged me to call her. I had been told that I would need a 5-ton unit which meant the price would be even more expensive than I had projected. After telephoning the business, I asked for an appointment and was given one. She remembered me from previous purchases and where I lived. I explained the reason for my visit which was a 5-ton heating and air conditioning unit. I wanted to know if her business had used ones that could be donated to me. She told me that 5-ton units were rarely available, that she did not have any in stock, but she would look around for one. She suggested that I call her in a week. When I called, she said, "You won't believe this. A local bank is replacing its 5-ton unit which was only a year old." The bank donated the unit to me. She gave me the information needed to have the unit installed and suggested that I call the vocational school to see if their students could install the unit. However, the vocational school could not accommodate me. The weather turned cold, so time lapsed.

During that time, I had no way of locking the doors, but I had not encountered any theft at the building. I had a board meeting. When I returned to the office, I discovered that someone had stolen the unit. I was livid. *God, what am I going to do?* When I returned home, I received a call from a church member telling me he saw a man with a cart carrying a large unit down the street. The caller thought the unit belonged to the church, so he followed the man with the cart. He described the house which was around the corner from the office. He told me to call the police which I did, and they told me to come down the next day to make a report. "Yea, right," I said. I put on my clothes. In doing so, Jeff called asking, "Are we writing tonight?" "No," I said. "I found out who has my heating and air conditioning unit, and I'm going to get it." "Wait Annette," he said, "I will call you back later." I hung up the phone. By the time I reached the door, Jeff appeared and said, "I'll go with you." We drove to the house. I jumped out of Jeff's suburban and went into the house. A man came to the door. "Where is my unit? I want it now," I said. He began to tell a lie about how someone *giving* it to him. "I don't care," I said, "I want my unit, and I want it now." He helped Jeff load the unit in his suburban and offered to help work on the building. I didn't accept his offer. The unit was installed by a gentleman for $100.

The building was coming together. The next urgent need was furniture. One of the board members at that time was an employee of a local bank. She told me that sometimes banks give old furniture to non-profits. She would inquire about the bank's donated furniture policy. The reply was that the bank no longer allowed groups to pick out the furniture, but she could. I was excited about the gift because the bank was known for superb decor. She called for us to come get the furniture. My face looked as if I could not believe it. The furniture was old, dusty, and mismatched. I didn't want to seem unappreciative, so I said "Thanks" with a big smile. While I was traveling to the office, I said, "Lord, I wanted some nice cherry wood, executive-style furniture." The men unloaded the furniture. As I sat alone, I heard the Spirit of God say, "Get some furniture polish."

"Okay." I replied, "but I'm not putting this in my office."

When I returned, I started cleaning the furniture. Led by the Holy Spirit, I placed certain pieces in different rooms. It was beautiful when I finished.

The interior of the building was appealing, but the outside had not changed. Propped up with a pulley and boards, it was still leaning. I believed siding would be less expensive than attempting to brick the place. I was given a name and a telephone number of a guy who hung siding. I called him and asked him to look at the project. A tall gentleman arrived at the house. From the window, I saw an expression of disbelief on his face. He looked as if he had driven to the wrong place. I met him and told him I needed siding put on the building. I also informed him I had no money.

He walked around the building and then stated, "You expect me to put my work on this thing." My feelings were hurt.

"Yes," I said.

He stated, "Do you know that it is leaning?" He chuckled, "I don't know. I will call you," he said.

When he left, I went inside the office and let the tears roll again. I called him back a week later. He came by and measured the building. "You need to get the materials," he shared. Still there was no money. I called the company that he suggested and asked if they could donate the materials. The office manager told me she would talk to the boss and call me back. Well she didn't, but I kept calling her every other day. I was informed the company could not donate the siding but had some discontinued items in stock which could be purchased at half price. I said, "Yes" but didn't know where the half price would come from. My son,

Corey, gave me the money and so the work started. Mr. Jackson and two of his employees worked on the building between their other jobs. I had no money but later learned that some days he paid for items from his own pocket. One day while working on the building, Mr. Jackson announced that he had closed his company and had office furniture and a conference table with leather chairs. He stated that I could use the furniture until he set up his new office. I declined because I wanted nothing to happen to the items under my care. Later, he decided to sell them to me for $500. I could pay when I collected the money. I saved every penny supporters gave me. When I finally had enough to pay him, I telephoned him to come and get the money. When he arrived, I unfolded the money from the desk draw. "Thank you for waiting," I said. "Oh keep it," he replied, "Maybe one day, you can help me." During this time, there were many people who came and helped to make TOPPS, Inc., a community location for families.

Chapter 4

<u>A TIME TO BE ALONE</u>

One would think the most comforting part of a journey is the portion in which you have someone to share the trip. I had to learn there are times when GOD WANTS YOU ALONE. That does not mean He doesn't allow family to be a part of your life, but he cuts off those who cannot go along. Sometimes people can become a distraction and a hindrance or cause us to become discouraged. To avoid being delayed, God often times will isolate us so that we are compelled to complete our mission.

At first, I did not understand. There were people I had helped, supported, and offered assistance to. I did whatever I could for them. The first people He disconnected me from were my close friends. They were people who I called my 'road lizards'. These were shopping buddies and telephone friends. At first, I thought they would be the type of friends I had been to them but *this* God-given project was different. God had me moving in a different direction. Just imagine trying to explain to another person that God doesn't want you to work, and you are going to lose a lot. They never visited me at the office or ever offered help - not even when I was "going through." The only words I would hear from them were "You will be alright." I could not afford to dine out, shop, or do the things I once did.

God wanted all of my attention. Even people I wanted to be in my life, God would say, "Not yet." In retrospect, I think about some of the people He removed. They would have never made the sacrifice I made. Some were absolutely selfish, and God wanted me to see their true character.

As I became a loner, I began to spend more time in the

presence of God. I found myself trying to listen to Him and learn how to follow His directions. My special day was one Sunday morning. I was getting dressed for church, and the Spirit said for me to go to my office. Lord, am I hearing you right, don't go to church? I never missed church unless it was very important.

I was obedient. When I arrived at the office, I sat down and said, "Okay, Lord. What now." I heard, "Praise Me." I put on some praise music, "Oh, it is Jesus," and then praying, and thanking God. As I worshipped God, the Holy Spirit filled the room. I heard the voice of the Lord say "There are things you have done that have totally pleased me." Then He showed me the things I had done for others that made Him proud (giving and helping people). There were things over the years He had instructed me to do. Then He said, "But let me show you what I'm not pleased with." As the images of my controlling attitude flashed before my eyes, I was so ashamed. There were people in my life He had sent and I was trying to be in control. The Lord reminded me that He would deal with those who misused TOPPS and took advantage of it. After I saw *myself, I* repented and asked God to help me help others in a more effective way. Later, I learned that wanting to control people is a form of *witchcraft*. God made me reap what I had sown. He put people around me who were awfully controlling. What I saw and heard was not something that I wanted to reflect, so I promised myself that I would change.

People are placed in your life for a reason and a season. How many times had I heard these words? It's cliché, but true

39

nonetheless. During my journey, I met a lady. When I was first introduced to her, she appeared to be much older than I. She had a scarf with a plastic cap on top. She was buttoned down as if it was below zero. Honestly, the only thing I had to say to her was "Hello." We worked out at the same gym. One day, I had been "going through" a terrible problem with the building and my personal life. She called me to share things only God knew. A few days later, she followed me to the office. As she entered the building, she told me things I had done and what God had said. We became close friends. As a matter of fact, we were prayer partners. I must admit, I depended on her; she would do special things for me. Sometimes she would pay to get my nails done. She would style my hair for free and then give me money. She taught me how to pray beyond what I knew. As problems intensified, so did our prayer life. We would pray twice a day—at 6:00 a.m. and at night.

The journey became even more difficult, so we increased our prayer time to three times a day. I depended on her for everything. She would tell me how God showed her that I would come into a lot of money and of course, being my friend, we talked about what I would do with the money. Mentally, I was drained from all I was going through, so I decided I needed to get away. I prayed and asked God if He would make a way for me to go on vacation for a few days. I found a complete trip, including a rental car, for $400. The door was opened for me to go to my favorite place which was Austin, Texas. This was also a networking opportunity, so I would be able to visit and get information on some other programs. I asked my friend if she wanted to go and she did, but did not know if her husband would approve. Then God told me to go alone.

God gave me these instructions. When I arrived, I was to cut off my cell phone and not to make any calls. I had not missed praying in a year with my friend, but I obeyed God. It was a beautiful time with God. He had me to get a notebook and write. I soaked in the tub, prayed and spent time with God. "Lord, are you going to allow me to go shopping?" I asked. My brother gave me a few dollars and it was burning a hole in my pocket. It had been so long since I was able to purchase anything that going to the *Dollar Store* had become a treat for me. The first two days, I was not able to shop, but I found time on the third day. I prayed and asked God where I should shop at. I know most people don't bother involving God with small details, but I do and will continue to. *Acknowledge Him in all of your ways, and He will direct your path.*

God pointed out a beautiful beige suit. The price was $64, but there was a smaller size on sale for $44. I went to the counter and asked why the larger one was not the same price. The lady gave me a sarcastic answer. In other words, "It's not on sale," she said. I was about to walk off when the Spirit instructed me to ask for the manager. I explained to the manager the problem. She checked the sales rack, and I purchased the suit for $24. Oh, by the way, I never wore the suit. I gave it to a young lady who God instructed me to give it to.

Also during the visit, God shared that my friendship was changing with my prayer partner. God prevailed on me to write her a letter. Even though I knew what God showed me about her was true, I refused to correspond with her. We continued to pray, but I knew that our rapport was exasperating. I ignored the signs God put before me. I caught her in untruths about things concerning other people who wanted to be a part of my life. She would tell me not to have anything to do with certain people. The prayers started focusing more on *getting* a blessing rather than *being* a blessing.

Finally one night, I received a telephone call. During the call, the person made a statement that I knew was referring to my *prayer partner*. "Everyone is not your friend," said the individual on the phone. I answered, "Yes, I know." Then, she enumerated information about my private life that I knew no one knew but my prayer partner. I didn't say a word. I became ill because everything the person said was true. How could my prayer partner share details about my personal business? How hurtful. When she called that night to pray, I told her that she had shared things about me that were hurtful. I cried for days. God showed me the devil can get to the people who are closest to you. I told her that night I forgave her, but we have not spoken since. I realized had I been obedient to the unction I received in the beginning, the relationship never would have led to such a disconcerting end, but a clearer picture to our purpose.

When one thing ends God always has a plan to bring along something new. As I became that loner again, there were times I could not muster enough energy to pray. One night, I called my sister, Pat. She and I grew up together, but over the years had differences of opinions on family issues. We would talk but not like sisters. We attended all family gatherings, but the relationship was distant. On that night, I called her and inquired about her family. As we talked, she asked about my friend. I told her what happened and she said, "You know, Net, I was jealous I would hear you talk about your prayer time, and I always wanted to pray with you." Pat and I became prayer partners and best friends. Every night and sometimes during the day, we would check on each other. It is amazing how we can live with a person all our lives and never completely know who the person is inside. I had robbed myself of a dear friend all those years. Pat was an encourager. She never had the material things in life like the rest of us nor did she ever desire them. She truly loved God. When she received anything, she shared. At this point in my life, I was destitute, and here it was I'm needing my sister who — really doesn't have it to give, to help me.

We formed a way of thanking God by saying "Glory" when something happened in our favor. She would answer the telephone saying, "God is Faithful." If I said, "Hey girl," she would say, "No,

Net, God is Faithful." I soon learned to say, "God Is Faithful." When we prayed, we would see visions at the same time. She never complained about not having enough as she sowed seeds for the future. In her prayers, she would always ask God to send my sister her Boaz. "Wait, Net, on your Boaz. We don't need any Ishmaels." Pat died August 2007. On the night before her death, we made our call to each other. It was late. I asked if she had talked to Willie, our brother. We made it a habit to all get on the telephone and pray as a family once a month. "No," she answered, "Call him." I answered her saying, "You know they go to bed early. It is 11:00 p.m." She said, "I am going to call my brother" and she did. Willie woke to talk with us. We all talked about the goodness of God and his *promises*. As always, we all stated what we wanted to pray about, and I started first. Pat prayed second, and her prayer was longer than usual. She read three scriptures God had placed on her heart to share about restoration. Then, Willie prayed. He was filled with the Spirit. It was a good time as we ended the call. She said, "Love you guys." I said out loud, "Pat didn't tell me she would talk to me tomorrow as she always did." It was the last time I talked with her. Sometimes, when I am down I hear her say, "Net, God Is Faithful."

Chapter 5

THE IMPACT ON MY PERSONAL LIFE

Committing to take on a mandate of this magnitude, also affected my mental state. Being a widow places you in a category that is difficult. To be honest, a feeling of shamefulness lingered over me, especially when I attended school functions. If they talked about children from single parent homes, I would become defensive. It was unfair to judge a person because of their marital status but I, too, had made these judgments. I now realize how difficult it was to have all the responsibilities of rearing children alone. The first six months after William's death, I lived a double life. During the day and at public places, I gave the appearance of being a strong widow who needed no help. However at night, I would lock myself in my room and cry myself to sleep. I would try hard for the children not to see me cry—and sometimes it was hard to hide. The first time I thought I was having a heart attack. I would bury myself in my work, for I had not left my job with HIPPY yet. The day of the first experience, I remember very well. It was on a Sunday afternoon. As I sat working, I had chest pains and was breathing hard. I called Corey and told him if I were not at home by 6:00 p.m., to come looking for me. Fear gripped my heart. I got down on my knees in my office. *Lord, what is wrong with me?* I was directed to look up the word "anxiety attack." It was at this moment that I realized I had areas in my life that I had not dealt with. Those locked chambers were affecting my life and I realized that I had covered my feelings up. *Anything covered can't heal.* I had just lost my mother a year earlier; William had passed; and now I faced not only leaving a job I loved but also losing my source of income.

I shared with my close friends, Pat and Jackie. Loneliness overwhelmed me. I thought about how William and I had just celebrated our 20th anniversary in October of 2000. I had never wanted to be single, and God knew this desire. Thus, I figured I wouldn't be single long. I remembered asking God about putting someone in my life. *Be careful what you ask God for!* He answered my prayer. I attended a program and on my way out I heard the Spirit say "Your husband will walk you to your vehicle." No one was outside, so I ignored what I had heard. By the time I walked to my truck, a young man said, "Hello, Mrs. Dove, how are you?" I was shocked, and all I could say was, "Oh! God, I don't want him!"

By now a year had passed since I prayed about God putting someone in my life. I used the track as a meeting place with God. One morning, I asked God again about someone with whom I could share my life. God reminded me that He had picked out a person for me, but I had said I didn't want him. "Who?" I asked God. But by that time I heard, "Hello, Mrs. Dove." The person whom God had showed me earlier was walking on the track right next to me. I knew nothing about him, but what I wanted and expected was absolutely not him.

Whenever we stumbled across one another on the track, we communicated. We became close friends, but the problem was that I still wasn't interested in him other than as a close friend. We shared nothing other than conversation about church and family.

Four months passed and God had told me to tell him he was my husband. I begged God not to require me to tell him this news. The Spirit would not let me sleep and would wake me up during the night until I agreed to be obedient. Monday morning came. I followed my routine—walking around the track. I knew I would see him there because he consistent with his morning exercise. *Oh Hallelujah!* He wasn't there that morning. So I felt I didn't have to say anything since he didn't show up. By now, I had done four laps. I looked up and there he stood at the gate. So as not to ignore him, I said, "You can't walk standing there."

"I can't I have injured my foot." He said.

I responded, "Then, why are you here"?

"I don't know", he replied.

But I knew, and I had to obey the spirit. *Please sit down.*

I said, "Now this is not me but God told me to tell you that you are supposed to be my husband." He got up and walked off without saying a word. Later, he called me and asked how long I had known about the proposal. I told him over two years. *By now he was engaged to be married to someone else.* I shared with him that I was not interested. He said, "I am scheduled to be married." I told him "that was good" because I did not like him. God revealed the purpose for my telling him. It was an answer to a question he had asked God.

TOPPS kept my focus, so I stopped thinking about someone being in my life. Time went by and a friend girl asked me if she could give a friend of hers my phone number. She said he was a widower. She described him as quiet, shy, tall, and thin. *Umm, sounds interesting.* I said, "Yes." I was excited. No one called me, and each Sunday she would ask me if he had called.

One Sunday in April 2004, my friend girl called saying, "*Hold* the phone." I did. The next voice I heard was the soft-spoken voice of a man on the other end. We talked about thirty minutes, and he asked if he could call me more. I agreed. We would talk for hours. I enjoyed the conversations. Then, he asked me if I would meet him and his son for pizza. I wasn't hungry, but I was curious about the person I had spent so much time talking to on the phone. It was like the first date. I dressed in a black suit— sure to look thinner than I was.

I arrived at the pizza restaurant. As I walked inside, I could not believe what I was seeing. There were only a few people in the room, so I assumed that the man sitting in the booth, was the person that I was there to meet. I dreaded approaching the table after noticing that this man had hair protruding out of his nose and ears. If that wasn't disappointing enough, he was unshaven, and completely not groomed. He wore overalls which were too short. *How could she do this to me, I kept thinking?* As they sat in a booth beside each other, I sat facing them, sitting on the edge of the bench. Unexpectedly, my daughter walked in to see whom I was meeting. I was very ashamed. She had a big smile on her face. I soon left. As I arrived at my car, I told God that I would not ask Him again about anyone being in my life.

The next day, I made up a big excuse and told him that I was not ready to date yet. He said, "That's okay. I'll be all right." I was sad because I didn't want to hurt his feelings. So I went to the florist and sent him a plant saying, "Thank you for three days of friendship." By the time I arrived at home, a large bouquet of flowers were waiting for me with a card saying, "Friends are forever."

We continued to talk as friends. I had never met a kinder gentleman in my life. He treated me like a lady. The problems I faced with TOPPS were not so great now. He would help me with repairs. He had been a widower for eleven years, and often allowed himself to be consumed with work.

By this time, I made a commitment to God to wait on Him to send me that special person. "God, I want to experience something special when I meet him." Two years passed. One day a friend whom I met in a beauty shop told me that she wanted me to meet her son. She was an elderly lady, and I was always taught to respect my elders, so I responded. "Okay," I said, with no intention of being interested. "My son, is here from Germany. He is a good man, he doesn't drink nor smoke, and he's good to me." She said. Being polite, I said, "That's good." She asked the proprietor to call for her ride home. A young lady walked into the beauty shop with a tall gentleman. I did not look because I thought the young lady was his girl friend. When the lady said, "Grandmother," I looked up. It felt as if my heart literally stopped beating. It scared me. She introduced him, but I could not stand to look at him, for fear of screaming.

"Lord, what happened," I thought to myself.

"That's what love at first sight feels like," He said.

On my way home the Spirit of God said "PURSUE". I can't "pursue". I was taught that women do not pursue men. God directed me to read the story of *Ruth*. Upon reading this book in the bible, I realized that Ruth had pursued Boaz. I didn't pursue him because I was afraid. His mother and I became very close friends. Presently, we talk daily. However, this area of my life has been put on hold until God is ready to move.

CHAPTER 6

UNDER ATTACK

One thing you learn when you commit to God's *Way* is that Satan will attack you in an effort to convince you to give in to his wiles. I have always been a persistent person. Giving up has never been an option. I have endeavored to be the best at what I attempt. However, during this journey I have cried more than ever before in my life. Before this community service trek, I have had some awful challenges. I thought everything would happen effortlessly especially since I was doing God's will. However, that was not the case. When satanic attacks are rejected, he increases his ammunition. Besides the financial ones, there were many other attacks that Satan attempted.

God Covered Me.

One of my part-time career jobs was selling lounge wear. The company was having a convention, and I wanted to attend, but I didn't have the funds for the trip. I had prayed and asked God to allow me to attend the last trip. In retrospect, He had instructed me to quit. My unit had earned more than $100,000 the first year, and I was scheduled to receive an award. I was able to book the flight on a credit card. I used another bank card to secure the hotel room. I had funds for food, yet I knew the company provided some of the meals.

On Wednesday, the day before I was scheduled to leave, I made a chart listing all tasks to be completed before boarding the flight. I needed to call West Memphis for our Delta Corp Volunteers and give them my report. I asked for Angela. When I first met her, I shared the "vision" God had given me. During the conversation about the report, she said, "The Spirit told me to pray for you and to bid you God's traveling favor." I answered her by saying, "I receive it." We concluded the telephone call, and I finished the remainder of my tasks on the chart.

Around 2:00 p.m., I received a telephone call from LaTunda. She was scheduled to travel to Boston, but had changed her mind. She proceeded to share that the airline I was taking just had a plane crash, and nineteen people were killed. She further shared her fears of flying. I wouldn't allow her message to claim my attention and mind. I ended the conversation by saying, "If I get killed while I'm going on this trip, it was nice knowing you. But I've already prayed about it." I went to the internet to pull up the story to find out why the plane crashed. I don't quite remember what all I had read, but I know that I had prayed.

Later that evening, Michael, my younger son, came to my bedroom while I was packing and told me that he felt this trip was different and in fact did not want me to travel. I stopped packing and started typing my last *Will and Testament*. My daughter, Raychelle, telephoned me asking what I was doing. When I told her "My *Will*," she became upset. "Why?" she asked. I replied,

"Well, I'm leaving tomorrow and with all that is going on, I rather have it done. So if you need it, it's here." She asked me not to talk like that. I read the *Will* to her. We laughed about the fact that I told her I had three children, and she wasn't my daughter. But of course, I was joking with her. She asked if she could have my bed. We laughed, and I hung up the phone. Next, I called Willie, my brother, who lived in Little Rock. I wanted him to be an advisor to the kids. Willie usually is never at home until late at night, but he answered the phone. I told him I was leaving for Boston and that I had completed my *Will*. He said, "Girl, you'll be fine." I said, "I know, but I'd rather have it." We talked a little longer and ended the conversation.

I finished packing, and then I felt the urge to pray. I told God I appreciated Him for making a way for the trip and to keep me safe. As I prepared for bed, I received a phone call from one of the people who was supposed to be traveling with me. The call was from Betty who told me that she would not be going, because her husband was uneasy about the trip. At that point, I said, "Okay" very curtly, and I laid back down. After a few minutes, I arose to pray again. This time, my prayer was, "Lord, I don't know what's going on, but if it's not for me to go on this trip, stop me from going. If it's my time, let me be prepared. But right now, I'm still going." (By this time, three persons had reversed opinions about traveling).

Corey, my older son, had driven to Pine Bluff from Little

Rock that night to drive me to the airport the next morning. I got up at 4:30 a.m. to get to the airport which was 45 minutes away. Betty called to tell me that she was joining me after all and she would meet me at the airport. As we entered the airport and proceeded to check in our luggage, there was only one person in line for our flight. After getting to the gate, others began to arrive. The flight departure was on schedule. I whispered a prayer as the small plane was being loaded. I hated to travel on a small plane. As we boarded, Betty turned to me and said, "If this plane crashes, we are dead because it's too small for us to get out." But nothing happened, and we had an excellent flight to Charlotte, North Carolina.

Our plane was scheduled to leave at 10:00 a.m. It was delayed to 12:00 noon, then to 1:00 p.m. "What was this?" we wondered. The plane finally came and we were successfully boarded. As it took off, I could hear *this funny noise*. I remembered looking at Betty and thinking, *"Is this it."* Then, we realized that it was just the sound of the aircraft. With beautiful weather and no problems, we landed in Boston. I thanked God out loud, then in my mind.

The convention was in session from Thursday through Sunday. It was a remarkable gathering. After arriving in our hotel room on Friday, I found ten messages on my phone. *What has happened now*? There was only one recorded message, and it was from Betty's husband. "Call home as soon as you get this message," he said. The message worried Betty. She had left her daughter, who had bad muscle spasms, with her husband. When she returned the phone call, her husband only wanted to know where to locate the grape juice they had purchased for Christmas. I called home. My house was full of people. Raychelle, Marcus, Michael, David, Kasee, Corey, Courteney, and Courtland were all doing fine.

I awakened the next morning realizing I had lived to be another year older. I thanked God for allowing me to see 47 years. On that Friday, I received three awards for unit sales of $100,000; personal sales of $100,000, and for 1,000 shows. The convention was coming to an end. I went into the bathroom and kneeled down by the tub to thank God for the trip and the awards—but mostly for the safety he had provided. I asked Him to take care of my home and to *see* us safely back home.

On Sunday morning we arose and dressed. Mamie, my sister-in-law, who had come to the convention was scheduled to depart around 10:00 a.m. She and I *went down* for breakfast and participated in the voting session. Betty came to breakfast later. Our flight was scheduled to leave at 4:30 p.m. With hours of leisure time before departing the hotel, we window-shopped, browsed the mall, and returned to the hotel room to get our luggage. Check out time was 1:00 p.m. Mamie had left earlier. Betty and I were in the hotel room. I told her I was going to pray and asked if she wanted to join me. She said, "Yes." I knelt by my bed and she knelt by her bed. We prayed and thanked God for another opportunity. I asked Him to see us safely home and to take care of our families.

We left for the airport. It dawned on me. At some point during our flight home, it would be night. I hated flying at night. I actually don't know why I have such fear of flying at night other than the fact that one can't see. We ran into a small amount of turbulence, but over all, it was a good flight home. When we landed in Little Rock we heard it had sleeted and snowed. I turned to Betty and said, "I've *gotta* get home so I can get my praise on for a safe trip." Betty answered, "You can thank God now!" And I did. "Be careful driving home," she instructed. I said, "I'll be fine."

Corey and Betty's husband were at the airport to meet us. While waiting on our baggage, Corey wanted to talk. I said, "Goodbye" to Betty and wished them well. Corey told me the ministry I had started at my church, (which involved picking up children and feeding them before Sunday school) was having some problems. Some of the officers at the church didn't want him to pick up the youth nor to get keys to the new church van. When he asked for the keys to the old van, he was told the vehicle had no gas in it. The children were picked up at 10:00 a.m. instead of 9:00 a.m. A new family of three accepted Jesus Christ and joined the church on that Sunday. As Corey and a friend walked me to my car, he asked if I could drive home safely. "Yes!" I told him, and that I was fine.

Satan tried to kill me!

On the way home, I called Raychelle to check on how things went, as I had left her responsible for feeding the children breakfast and lunch after church. She told me she had experienced problems with letting the children eat. When I hung up the phone, the more I thought about the situation, and the more it grieved my spirit. My displeasure was Christians were fighting the good things we were trying to do for God, which was outreach ministry. I was told at a meeting the following Wednesday night a lady said I shouldn't be feeding those children. They could eat at home. I became furious thinking about this present dilemma. I recognized this as an attack of the enemy, so I turned on Yolanda Adams' song entitled, "The Battle Is Not Yours, It's the Lord's" and praised God.

I felt a tightness in my chest—which was anxiety. I told the devil he was a liar about TOPPS and about the outreach ministry (the kids). "No weapon formed against me shall prosper." I repeated that twice. As I said the words again, I crossed over a bridge, and lost control of my car. It began spinning frenziedly; I could do nothing. I glanced quickly viewing a deep ditch filled with tall pine trees and it seemed as though I was headed toward them. The car was on two wheels by now, ready to turn over. I did not have my seat belt buckled. I shouted hysterically, "JESUS

SAVE MY LIFE... JESUS SAVE MY LIFE!" Frantically, I screamed at the top of my voice. I took my hand off the steering wheel and it seemed as though the vehicle moved faster. The car was spinning recklessly and moving chaotically toward the median. Finally, the car stopped in the middle, between the two highways. I sat there saying, "God saved my life."

I dialed *911* to inform them about the incident. Unexpectedly, my phone began to fade out. The *911* operator told me it would be awhile before the arrival of an officer. A White Hall policeman came along and asked me if I was okay. I told him what happened. He looked at the skid marks on the highway. My car had no damage! He called for a wrecker. Standing by my car and waiting for the wrecker, we saw a gray truck traveling over the bridge. It began to spin as my car had done. In a moment, control was lost and the truck went speedily into the embankment and crashed. We could hear the travelers screaming. I began running and calling on the name "Jesus" Oh! "Jesus." The Spirit let me know that had I crashed earlier on this stretch of highway, no one would have seen the accident. Had we not been there when the truck crashed, the officer and I would not have seen this latter incident. The embankment was just that deep.

After waiting two hours, my car was pulled out of the median. I asked about the people in the gray truck and was told by the officer they were going to be okay. I drove home. The Spirit told me that Satan was trying to kill me. Thanking God, I said,

"Satan was defeated." When I arrived home my daughter, Kasee, had purchased a birthday cake with a photo of us. We were born on the same day. I hugged her and went to my room to get my praise on. Throughout the night and the next morning I thought about how the devil was trying to kill me. I promised him—the devil— that I was going to call everyone I knew to tell them how God saved my life. I did just that.

One of the people I called was Nina— one of my cousins. After telling her what happened, she thanked God, and we hung up. Later that day, she called back and asked me what color was the truck I saw that had crashed. I told her gray. She asked me, "Where did it happen?" I told her the location. She then told me that the driver was a member of her church, Sister Freddie's daughter. Sister Freddie was a member of the board of directors for TOPPS.

Sickness

When I left my job at *HIPPY* I was responsible for my health insurance. I was taught insurance is an essential protection. I started paying $363.00 a month for a health policy. When my income decreased I had to allow my policy to lapse. I was nervous because I had high blood pressure and diabetes had been detected.

The first attack came during the morning when I was preparing to leave the house. Michael came into my room and fell to the floor. He was in pain. I rushed him to the hospital. After Xrays, the physicians could not find anything. A similar incident had happened before. The specialist referred him for tests. Nothing unusual was found. The bill totaled over $2,000. I could not afford to pay it.

The second attack came when I was having some problems. I went to the doctor where my old insurance information was a part of the file. After examining me, he said, "You need to see a specialist right away." The nurse started to call the referring doctor when I informed them I did not have insurance. I asked to be referred to the state hospital. My appointment was scheduled six months later. I wondered for six months whether or not stress could weigh in as a problem. *Is this what people experience when they do not have insurance?* All I could do was pray, "Lord, I'm committed to you with no insurance; take care of me." When I went in for my next visit, they began running tests on my kidneys.

The most serious attack came one night when I was sitting in church and I received a message that my sister had been taken to the hospital (she lived 45 miles away). She had had a heart attack. When we arrived at the hospital, the doctors informed us they had to shock her back twice. It did not look good for her. Ministers from her church were standing around praying. My brother and my sister's husband began to hold hands and pray. The physicians allowed the family to visit her. She was not responding. We had a cousin who worked in the hospital. She called me into the hallway and said, "Pat is not going *to make* it." She was crying. "That's not what God told me", I said. The doctors informed us they were going to transfer her to another hospital which was more equipped for her needs. The concern was she would probably not survive the ride. It was sleeting outside. We all loaded into one car and proceeded to the other hospital. It took the ambulance a very long time to arrive.

We assembled in the family room. The doctors came in with the report which revealed she had lost oxygen and would not live until the next morning. We were given permission to visit her. We were all upset. I left to enter the chapel in order to talk to God. "God", I said, "I need a favor. I do not care about what I've been asking you to do. I need my sister. Please allow her to live." We sat around all night. The next morning we went in to see her. She was still not responding. All of a sudden she jerked! We felt hopeful, so we called the nurse who said she *would do that* which was normal. I heard God say, "Begin to pray." We all joined hands and started praying. Pat opened her eyes and started trying to talk. The doctors said she would be brain dead. Not only was she not brain dead, but she worked with children's ministry weekly in her neighborhood until her death. Thirteen people gave their lives to God at her funeral.

Mind Battles

There were times during this journey when Satan worked overtime—it seems—on my mind. I recollect that one day I was sitting in the office. He began to taunt me by asking me if I remembered when I traveled, shopped, and purchased nice clothes. He said, "Look at you now. Your clothes don't fit. You're broke. You don't have a man in your life." I started crying. My world appeared as if I had failed.

I received a call from a family member asking me if I was sure I heard from God. The concern was I needed to get a job. I thought about it and shared, "No, I'm sure I heard from God." But, I thought to myself, why be things so difficult. That night I prayed, "Lord, please deliver me from the pain." I needed money and I needed to see God move—nothing appeared to be working. *Be still and know I am God. No matter what it looks and feels like, just praise Me.*

I had many attacks on my mind but I was able to combat the assaults with a song and the Word of God. The strongest attack came in September 2006. I came home from church service. I had joined another church by now. Service was good and as usual God's presence was there. I began to ponder the fact that I had received a notice my house was being foreclosed. Where would I go? My mother's house needed so much work. The devil began his attacks again by saying, "If you are serving God, why would He let you lose your house? He has left you and your credit is bad. You've been sued by four companies and the Veterans Administration has sent you a letter informing you that your benefits have been cut to $3.83 a month. You need to shut down

TOPPS and go get a job."

I cried all over again. The time was 6:15 p.m. At 11:00 p.m. I was still crying. Well, I said, "Guess I'll look for a job and file bankruptcy." Then I began reading the Word of God. *"Jesus Saves!"* I read it five times. I jumped up and said, "HELL NO! I'm not quitting, I'm not filing bankruptcy, and I will not look for a job." When you are in debt, people you owe will talk to you as if you are nothing. I was told you need to go get a job. Sell your home. What did I expect? On the last day to get the mortgage paid, I received a call from the same man who had talked crazily before. *Lord I don't feel like hearing this today.*

The man said, "Mrs. Dove, I am trying to help you."

"Yes," I said.

He said, "I am going to lower your payments, drop your interest rate, pay your taxes, and your next payment is due in two months."

I praised God until I could not talk. There were months when my life seemed to turn upside down. I had started talking with a former family friend about my journey. He was one of William's best friends and did not have a relationship with God. I believed that I could encourage him to seek after God. He was wealthy. As a matter of fact, when William died, he offered to pay off all of the debts we owed. I refused the offer. There were days I hated I did but now I thank God I never accepted. He was a very smart man but controlling. He had a rough life growing up and his mother was abusive. There was a hidden anger issue I felt he had against women. He offered to be Mike's godfather. Not consulting God, I allowed Mike to decide. He shared some very good information, yet he expected me to do whatever he suggested. He felt giving up my job was a crazy act. When I shared what "God" had said, he would make statements such as, "He's probably telling you to go get a job and you are too stupid to hear him."

I purchased a 2001 S Type Jaguar the year following William's death. I was still working and traveling and had put more than 90,000 miles on the car. It had started giving me trouble. By this time, I decided since I was not working I would attempt to sell it. God told me to clean the car. I removed all discarded papers from the back and front seats. "No!" I heard the Spirit say, "The entire car. I'm preparing you for a new car." I opened the trunk and took everything out. I was so excited. If you can recall, I had used my car note to buy supplies, so I was two notes behind. I would pay one note to keep from getting three months behind.

Our family friend was coming to town to bring Michael a graduation present. God had shared with me that he wished to help me get another car. He had mentioned a couple of times about my trading the vehicle in but my credit was not good.

When he arrived in town we went to meet Michael and

made plans for dinner. Following dinner, he told me I needed to give this nonsense up about TOPPS and get a job. I was getting angry but I could hear the Spirit say, "Just be quiet and let him talk." I remained silent until he said, "This faith thing is a bunch of [*curse word*]."

I fired off! "You don't tell me about my God and I don't care who doesn't think it's real. I'm not getting a job." He left Pine Bluff without anymore words.

Two day later I woke up earlier than usual. "Go to the track," I heard the Spirit say. At 6:00 a.m. I left. When I arrived there and started walking I began talking to God. I told Him that I know I heard him tell me to open TOPPS. I remember thinking, *"God, I know you have said don't work but I feel my needs are not being met. I owe everyone."* All I could hear was, "Trust Me".

When I arrived at the office that morning I had five calls on my phone from home. *"What has happened now?"* I thought. I returned the call to Kasee. She said a man had been to the house with a wrecker truck to pick up my car and had left his number. I called. He told me he was there to pick up my car. I told him I was at my office and he could come there to get it—which he did. It did not affect me at that time, because I knew I could not afford the notes or the repairs that were needed on the car. I began to thank God for another vehicle. I went on with my work that day. At 5:30 p.m. I received a knock on the office door. There stood a man who had the appearance of a homeless person.

"Hey Lady, I'll cut your yard for you."

"Sir," I said, "I don't have any money."

He said, "What about $5.00."

I told him I didn't have $5.00.

He said, "What about $2.00."

I told him I did not have $2.00.

"Well," he said, "Give me a dollar."

"Hold on," I said, "Let me look." Sometimes I had spare change in my purse or in my office drawer. I found about 35 cents. I went back to the door and said, "Sir, I don't have a dollar but if you come back tomorrow I will have it."

I had a water bottle that I kept change in at home and I would be able to get some money for him. When he left, I begin to cry. I told God, "That's why I'm here to help people and I can't even help him with a dollar." That night, I had six dollars in the water bottle. I took it to the office and he showed up. Every week for two months he came by the office and cut the grass for whatever I had. One day I decided to invite him inside the office and talked with him. I started out by asking, "Are you taking money to get something to drink?" He smiled and said he was getting something to eat. Then I asked, "Do you go to church?"

"Yes", he replied. I asked him what church he attended. He could not think of the name of the church. Then he asked me why I was inquisitive about him. Was it that I wanted him to attend my church? I told him that if he had a church already, that it was fine.

As we talked, he began sharing his life's story. He was living up North when he got into trouble that caused him to be in Pine Bluff. I asked what kind of trouble he had gotten into and he dropped his head and tears began to fill his eyes as he told me. He was married and had two children. He had a good job. He went on to say one day a friend who was homeless came to him for help. He allowed him to stay with his family. It wasn't long before he learned the man was having an affair with his wife. He became angry and beat the man severely. He went to jail for six months.

While he was in jail the man lived in his house. He said all he could think about was missing time with his kids, not being there for their birthdays, and losing his job. On the day of his release from jail he beat the man again, almost killing him. He was arrested again the same day. As he sat in jail he knew he was facing some time in prison. So, he prayed and asked God to let him go and he would leave. When he went before the Judge he pled, "Guilty." The Judge told him she was going to give him one more chance. He left that day and came to Pine Bluff where his father and sister lived.

His father died a year later. He began to cut yards to take

care of himself. I asked why for such a small amount. He answered me by saying he did not want to cheat anyone. One day he asked me how old I was. I told him that he wasn't supposed to ask a lady her age. He smiled and said, "You look pretty good for your age." Sometime I see him walking down the street. (*How blessed we are.*)

THE FEELING OF WORTHLESSNESS

I am writing about the feeling of worthlessness because I have been made to feel this way by so many people. Yes, it is true that when individuals have money and insurance, society sees them as someone of importance. When I was employed, I had all the benefits that society deemed necessary to live a worthwhile life. But my income declined and all my benefits left. I could no longer pay $363 a month for insurance for my family and myself.

At first, I worried because I was always taught by my Mom that a person must always have insurance. In reality, I paid out so much in insurance that one could say that I was insurance-poor. I still didn't have enough. I was no longer able to afford to go to the doctor or even purchase my medication. I had high blood pressure, diabetes, and was prescribed a hormone regiment. There were times when I would have to skip taking my medicine for a day in order to make the medication last.

Once a year, I scheduled an appointment to see my doctor, but the bills would be more than I could afford. I never left her office with less than $100 for the visit which did not include the lab work. She always felt like I purposely refused to follow her instructions. That was not the case. I knew I could not afford the bill and in a few months they would send it to collections. I never forgot the day I thought it was a blessing when I ran into a friend from school, who told me her agency should provide my medications but my doctor would have to sign the form.

I was so excited. Now, I could finally take the medications I needed every day. So I called the doctor's office and asked for the nurse and left a message about what I wanted. She returned the call to tell me the doctor stated she could not sign any forms for me to get medicines because I refused to come in on my regular visits. I had missed my August appointment and it was now the month of September. I explained that I did not have insurance and could not afford the fee for a visit.

The response was, "Well, I'm sorry."

I hung up feeling worthless. *"Dear God,"* I prayed, *"I hope she has to never experience what I am going through. How many times have I been insensitive to people?"*

CHAPTER 7

RAINDROPS OF BLESSINGS

I love my children more than words could ever express. Before starting this journey all of the children were at home. Corey, the oldest, had returned from Dallas trying to be closer to his daughter. Raychelle had graduated from a two-year college and the pressure seemed to over take me. One night, I wrote a letter to the two older children asking them to move out on their own. I didn't give them the letter but they soon moved to Little Rock. Kasee and Michael were left at home. William and I had provided a pretty good life for our children. As a matter-of-fact we helped with so many needs, especially those of other children. I explained to Michael and Kasee things such as our present economic woes. Things would be different when grants started coming in and I could pay myself. We would be back where we were. I had no idea what was to come. After losing my income, we lived on Mike's benefits from his father. Kasee had a part time job but it wasn't enough to help out. William and I had purchased all of our children cars. Mike had been promised a car when things got better. I knew with the grant I wrote with the group that offered me $200,000, I would get a nice salary. When I learned I was not getting the grant I wanted to figure out how to avoid having to tell him. On the way to school that morning, he had asked if we could go by the store. There were days when I did not have two dollars to give him. He

plan.

Eventually grants came in: $1,000 for books; $1,500 for a computer; and $5,000 for programs, materials, and office supplies. Dedril, who had worked for me at *HIPPY*, decided to give up her job and work with me. I told her that I could not guarantee anything. Dedril (Dee) came on board. We received the *Robert Wood Johnson* grant. With all the financial hardships, I looked forward to the salary, but God instructed me to give the funds to Dee in the form of a salary. We were blessed with twenty-six volunteers and fifty clients.

My son, Corey, was a blessing. He assisted me with the bills at home. I knew he could not afford to help, but when he did, God would bless him double-fold, in return.

HOLD OUT

I'm sure you've thought *why didn't I just quit, locate a job, or get my life back?* To tell the truth, I wonder it too. I made a vow to go back to the community. What made me push forward with such passion was an episode which happened at my old church. On the fifth Sunday in May 2002 as I prepared to minister a word from the Lord, the *Presence of God* was in the building. I lifted my hands and said, "Lord, I surrender my life to You." I had already committed my Life to Him. There were many times in which I wanted to quit, but the word, "Surrender, " came to my mind. I am not a quitter. My birth mother would tell me, "When things get hard, you can do it." I remember working on my Master's degree. I drove to Arkadelphia every day. The last week was quite chaotic. I was taking research, and it was hard. I started to quit. Mother called me and said, "Net, you can do it. Don't quit." I had not told her; she just knew. I would call friends who were strong in the Lord and tell them to pray with me. Some people whom God had planted along the way would call me when I was going through and say, "You were in my spirit. You are going to be alright." After Pat passed, I could hear her words, "Net, God is faithful." There would be times at night when I would ball up in fetal position and cry hard. I was not only crying for me but for what my children had to endure.

CHAPTER 8

<u>LEARNING TO HEAR, OBEY, AND DISCERN</u>

In July, only weeks had passed since the incident about my car when the Spirit of God said, "It's time for you to leave your church."

"Oh, no!" I said, "I know I didn't hear that."

I shut down, trying not to hear anything. I would not even pray unless it was with my prayer partner and I would not ask for any directions.

Every morning I would say, "God order my steps." For almost a week, I would say nothing about his *will* or directions. I was afraid. I would cry at night, "Please, don't let it be so."

You see, I grew up in this church. Mom and Dad, grandmother, all my friends, and people who would pray for me were members.

"Why, Lord?" I asked.

"Just trust me," he said.

One day I was stranded at home. *Now I know God purposed it to happen.* I was mowing the yard, walking and crying. "I don't want to leave," I said repeatedly. I had not slept completely in a week, so I decided to *surrender* to God's will.

"Okay, Lord," I said. "I need a sign if this is what I am hearing you say." I went into the house from mowing the yard. I sat down on the couch and turned on the television. The *Joyce Meyers Program* was being aired. She was preaching about the time when God told her to leave the church she was attending. My eyes got big as saucers. I knew the answer.

I called the pastor and told him I needed to talk with him about my leaving the church. God had already told me the people would not understand, but I wanted to leave the church in a decent and orderly way. On the Sunday morning in which I decided to tell the church, I was nervous. I got dressed, kneeled by the bed, and said, "Lord, I need another sign. I love my church." There was no answer from God. I went downstairs and turned on the television to check the time. T.D. Jakes was preaching on the focus point of *when God asks you to leave your church.* That was my confirmation. I arrived at church and went to look for the pastor. He was not in yet. I sat in my Church School class until he arrived. He passed by me, not even making eye contact. I stood up, went to him, and asked to speak with him for a minute or so. We went into his office and I began to explain all.

He said, "Uh, where are you going?"

I told him that I did not know for sure. I asked permission to make a statement before the church.

He answered, "Okay." He shared further that I was

welcome to come back home. The conversation ended. When morning service was ending, he stood, telling the congregation, "Sis. Dove would like to make a statement." The Spirit kept saying to thank everyone who helped to raise me and supported me. I also told them that I always thought I would die a member of this church, but God had said differently. I asked for their prayers and to be welcomed back if God says so.

That night, my daughter who lived 45 miles away called to tell me that she had heard that I left the church because someone made me mad. The next day, I received a call saying they heard I was involved with a man in the church. The last lie I heard was I had stolen money from the church. *People did not understand* as God had said.

The next Sunday I woke up asking God where He was going to send me. I had visited Canaan before, but never considered joining there. My friend had invited me. I arrived at the church but did not see her car. I decided to leave when the Spirit said, "Go in." I went in to sit in the back. The small congregation was standing with their hands up. I was uncomfortable because where I worshipped, we did not give praise and worship in that manner. The minister started preaching. It appeared that he knew everything God had said to me. I sat there with tears streaming down my face. I could not control the tears.

I visited Canaan again the next Sunday and the same thing

happened again. "Lord, what is this?"

"This is where I want you to be," He said.

I had visited Canaan in 2001 when the congregation had meetings in their home for Bible study. I planted a seed of $100 with the intent of never returning.

The third time I attended the church, I joined. I thank God for what I have learned and the teaching of who I truly am in Christ Jesus. I believe that I had to learn to warfare for the journey that was set before me. I was also sent to work in the church. At the beginning, I wrote about a friend who would always share how God would speak to her. I wanted that same type of relationship. It was not clear to me how it was possible. I would hear ministers say God doesn't talk to you. I purchased books about learning the voice of God, but nothing was clear until I began praying.

Spending time in the presence of God - what does that truly mean? *Talking to God, praising Him, letting Him know how much I appreciate everything He has done for me, and developing a love relationship with Him* were focus points. There were times during the journey I could not figure out if it was my thoughts or the Holy Spirit so I would constantly ask for the Holy Spirit to direct me. I would write items on my daily assignment chart such as "Order My Step." Even while praying, I would utter, "Let my thoughts be your thoughts, O Lord." If I was unsure I would repent for not being sure and wait until I was sure of what to do. I do believe sometimes I missed blessings. There were lessons I had to repeat because I did not seek God as I should have.

I learned that my mouth was the key to my faith working quickly. It was easy to tell my children and friends to watch what you say, but I would speak faith and then turn around and point out all the negative things. Every time something happened, I had to stop reacting or allowing the devil to "make a run on me." In other words, I had to stop crying, complaining, worrying, or stressing out, but speak God's word, or as I would say, "God's got this." I learned that attacks are to get you off focus. If you spend time complaining, you can't praise God for what is to come. I learned even to thank Him in advance. When I became worried about not having funding, I remembered the days when I had no floors and walls. I would go to the office, walk through every room and thank God for the beautiful walls, carpet, furniture, and people. *It came to pass.*

My relationship with God was a personal one. Early mornings, I would get these *'wakes'* to come pray or go to the office and *steal away*. I could hear so clearly when I complied with His directions. In obeying God, there were times I would do things knowing that I heard the voice of God, but nothing was there. For example when asked, "Go to the mailbox," I would drive across town to find that it was empty. The natural man said, "You didn't hear God." I began reasoning. I learned that obedience is what God was testing even when you don't see anything. The Spirit said, "Will you trust me?" So if it happened, I would return with *"obedience is better than sacrifice"* and realize that it's coming. *I love God. I truly love God.* There was much that I did not understand but I trusted Him.

A friend once told me that he would get a chair and sit it in front of him and invite God to sit and talk to him. I did it, feeling *His presence* was there. When the journey became tough, I would get on my knees in my room and lay my head in my desk chair and the presence of God's hand was on my head as a child in their father's lap. A peace would overtake me and sometimes I would awaken from a very relaxing sleep. As I pray for wisdom, I have grown tremendously in discerning the things of God. People can make appointments with me, and I can clearly hear when they are lying, or God will tell me whether or not I should help them, or just pray for them.

CHAPTER 9

THE PROMISES

EVERY PROMISE IS YEA AND AMEN

Throughout the journey, I constantly reminded God of *His Promises*. Many *Promises* were given by men and women of faith to be given to me. Then, there were *Promises* given directly to me. I would record some when they were given through prophets. The first *Promise* just before my journey started was given by Reverend Dr. Hazel Linton. She is a professor at the university, a minister, my mentor, and a person I admire. When William died, she came to the house. She had to have felt my pain. Before leaving, she asked if she could pray. As she prayed, I felt the Spirit of God through her words as she finished praying. She looked me in the eyes and uttered, "God said He is going to bless you for all that you have done. *Baby you've planted*," I was told by three men and women of God; "it will happen very soon."

Another *Promise* God gave me directly was a recipe. It was on Thanksgiving Day 2002 when I was *baking* a pie, I heard the Spirit so clearly tell me to add another ingredient. I said, "I don't like that. Sweet potato pies are my favorite and I don't want to mess it up." I heard the Spirit again, so I obeyed. After it finished baking, I asked my sister and brother to taste the pie because God said it will make *millions*.

The last *Promise* I will share — is this book. During the journey, I was instructed to write down the things that happened to me. I was told it would be a best seller. I would write, then stop, because the journey became so tough that it seemed too hard to bear.

Many seeds were sown and God knows every last one of them will bear fruit. One of the ministers who served on my Board called one day and said, "I need to talk to you. God said for you to write in your check book the amount of money you want." I was so broke that ten dollars would have been good. I wrote $100,000. The minister told me that the same amount I wrote, that God was going to provide. Mom (Mother Clardy), often called especially when I was down to say, "You are going to be blessed, Net. Just hold on. You will have money with no strings attached." After joining Canaan, every Sunday it seemed as if Pastor Banks would speak a *Word* directly to me. One Sunday, he told me that God wanted to know how much I wanted. I knew what had been stolen—millions, and I wanted it all returned. He told the entire church to write down what God said, "That I would be worth millions, not a million but millions."

People I did not know came by the office for unusual reasons. One day, I had comforters sitting on the porch and a minister stopped with two ladies and one young man to look at them. I had met him before, but he did not remember me. As they asked about the comforters, he asked my name. He said they had heard about me and tried to locate me. He told me God showed him some of the men who would come to help me with the project and they would be professional men. Then, there were prophecies given to others and the ones I hold so dear to my heart. One morning on my walk around the building, I remember asking God when *TOPPS* would be fulfilled. As I began to praise Him for what He had already done, I heard the Spirit say, "Look up."

"Look up?" I asked.

"Yes, into the sky," the Spirit said.

As I stopped walking and looked into the sky, the biggest bird I had ever seen had its wings spread out. "Watch it," the Spirit said. It began going up, up, and up until it disappeared. "You are going to soar just like that bird." I will never forget that day.

One night I was praying about *TOPPS*. I wondered why I couldn't do things for the neighborhood like it needed to be done. We were running out of space, the building was congested with kids. I kept crying out to God. I went to bed only for God to awake me to tell me to put my vision for the building I wanted on paper. So I drew a sketch of the building, "But where God," I asked. The next night, I was given the location and five men who would help to build the complex.

There are days I ask God, "When will these things come to pass?" and then I think about where He actually brought me from.

The devil tries to get me to focus on what was before the journey, but I put my faith in what is to come.

For those of you who find yourself with *Promises* from God, hold on until they come to pass. Each day, I continue to hold on. I believe God; that His promises will manifest in my life.

CHAPTER 10

<u>THE FINISH LINE</u>

I cannot help but think of the many obstacles and thoughts that go through the mind of a person who is close to the *finish line*. For me, trying to keep focus is the hardest thing to do. Often times, I find myself facing new obstacles each day. Sometimes it becomes overwhelming, but I am learning to not be easily distracted. I stand on the word of God when things seem impossible, believing the report of the Lord. *We are victorious in Christ Jesus.*

One day you may be excited and positive, but the next day the attack may intensify. The weapons are formed, but you must know that they shall not prosper. I often speak about the promises of God. My life has changed drastically. To go from having more than enough to having to deal with bill collectors, garnishments, shut-off notices, and no prospect of money would leave one to wonder *who do I trust, now?*

I want to encourage you to stand firm on the promises of God. When I feel discouraged, I listen to songs of encouragement, such as: *Encourage Yourself, The Battle Is Not Yours; it's The Lord's, Victory Is Mine, and Your Latter Will Be Greater Than Your Past.*

There are times in my life, when the enemy will try to remind me of how my life could have been different financially. I think about how I wouldn't have some of the struggles that I've experienced had I stayed on my job. Nevertheless, when I see a young man or woman whom I have helped, and I hear them speak about the impact that I've had on his or her life… it makes it all worthwhile. I am use to the *finer* things in life, so needless to say, this has been a humbling but rewarding experience.

I am getting close to the finish line. How do I know that the finish line is ahead? I've learned that when victory is nearby, things and people will shift around you. Imagine a basketball game. It's the fourth quarter, and there's three seconds left. The home team is down by one point. They pass in the ball. At this point, the opposing team has maximized their defense. The player catches the ball, he shoots, and scores two points. The buzzer goes off and the team and all of their fans cheer for joy. It is said that "it's always darkest before dawn". It is right when you are at the edge of your breakthrough that the enemy intensifies his defense tactics. He will do anything to try to steal the ball or block the shot. He doesn't want to see you succeed, but greater is He that is in *you* than he that is in the world. Don't allow his opposition to cause you to forfeit your victory. Take the risk, trust in God, and know that you have been predestined to reign. Increase your prayer life, and elevate your praise.

There's an old saying that says "When praises go up, blessings come down." I combat these attacks with the word of God, and my faith in knowing that all things will work together for my good.

People begin to surround you and tell you to keep going:

Sometimes on this type of journey, you feel isolated. While you're going through your wilderness experience, usually (like me), you have to take the walk alone. It's hard to find someone to lift you up. This is the time when God wants your undivided attention, so he often causes communication to fall off with our peers and in my case, as you read, even our close friends. So, when He allows people to come to me with words of encouragement—just what I need to hear to encourage me to stay the course.

There is a sound of victory in the air.

I can literally *feel* when something good is about to happen in my life. I know that God is getting ready to restore everything that has been stolen from me. Everything that has been locked up, I believe that God is releasing it now. I have yet to see the full manifestation, but consistently, God showers me with small blessings, reminding me that something greater is on the way.

God performs His Word.

You've witnessed God making provisions in my life throughout this book. When I get discouraged and I feel like things are not moving forward in my life, I think about how God performs His word in my life. I've often heard the saying "the race is not given to the swift or the strong, but to those who endure until the end."

This is why I continue to press toward the mark of the high calling in Christ Jesus. I figure, I've already been at my lowest, why not wait for my victory. Waiting is a process that requires patience. This has been a long journey. It has not been easy at all, but I have learned many things throughout this experience. It took me many years to complete this project, but God reminded me that there is more to come. If I wait on the Lord and be of good courage I believe that I shall walk in victory. After all, God did promise me that if I don't grow weary, and if I stay the course, there will be a *Victory in Waiting.*

ABOUT THE AUTHOR

Founder of TOPPS, Annette Dove, also serves as the Chief Executive Officer of the nonprofit organization. Dove academic background consist of a Bachelor of Science Degree in Special Education K-12, a Master of Science Degree in Education, an Elementary Education Administration Certification, an Arkansas Teacher's Certificate, and a TAPP (Training Arkansas Profession Pathways) Certificate as a State Trainer. Dove also has over 30 years of experience working directly with youth.

Dove has taught in the Pine Bluff school district for 11 years, 11 years as the director of the federally funded program "Home Instruction Program for Preschool Youngster (HIPPY), served 12 years as the church youth director, and multiple years on the Early Childhood Commission. Originally the idea to start an organization like TOPPS was the idea of Annette and her late husband William Dove. William passed away in 2000, after taking some time to think about how to make their dream happen, Annette retired from her director role at HIPPY and started the TOPPS journey.

Journey is certainly the best way of describing TOPPS for Dove. Dove has seen the highs and lows while working to fulfill her dream. Dove has used all of her savings, stock investments, retirements, and even filed bankruptcy to ensure the TOPPS doors stay open. However, TOPPS and Dove was the highlight story on NBC's making a Difference with Bryan Williams. Dove had the privilege of being interviewed by Chelsea Clinton, in her debut story on NBC. TOPPS garnished widespread attention and great responses from thousands across the country. No matter how tough the journey gets, Dove has consistently relied on her faith to keep persevering for the children of her community. Dove dreams of the day TOPPS will have a brand new center, so that TOPPS will be able to adequately provide more services for children all over the city.

Annette Dove
TOPPS INC.
Targeting Our People's Priorities with Service
Executive Director